BRYSON'S
BIG ADVENTURE

My First Year

By: Kendra Carter
Illustrations: Surplus Stephens

Archway Publishing books may be ordered through booksellers or by contacting:

Archway Publishing
1663 Liberty Drive
Bloomington, IN 47403
www.archwaypublishing.com
1 (888) 242-5904

Interior Image Credit: Surplus Stephens

ISBN: 978-1-4808-83932 (sc)
ISBN: 978-1-4808-8394-9 (e)

Print information available on the last page.

Archway Publishing rev. date: 10/15/2019

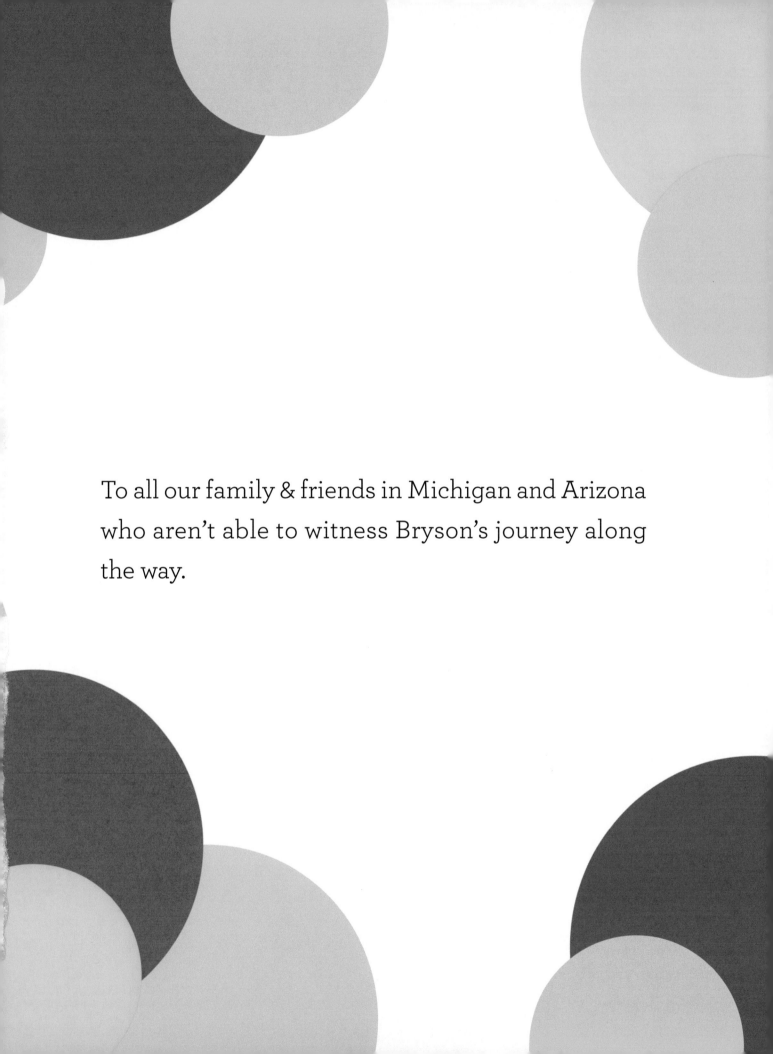

To all our family & friends in Michigan and Arizona who aren't able to witness Bryson's journey along the way.

Hi guys, it's me...Bryson Gregory Melvin. Yeah don't laugh; I'm the kid with three first names. I'm not really sure what my parents were thinking, but they swear I'll thank them later.

So I came into this world on a nice hot day, May 11th 2018 in the city that never sleeps...Las Vegas. I'm not really sure what that means not to sleep because I slept so much when I came into the light. And why is the light so bright anyway? Word of advice for you big people: can the lights be dimmed a little for my future friends that are coming into the world? I mean geesh, don't you notice us squinting our eyes before that yucky gunk stuff is placed all over them?!

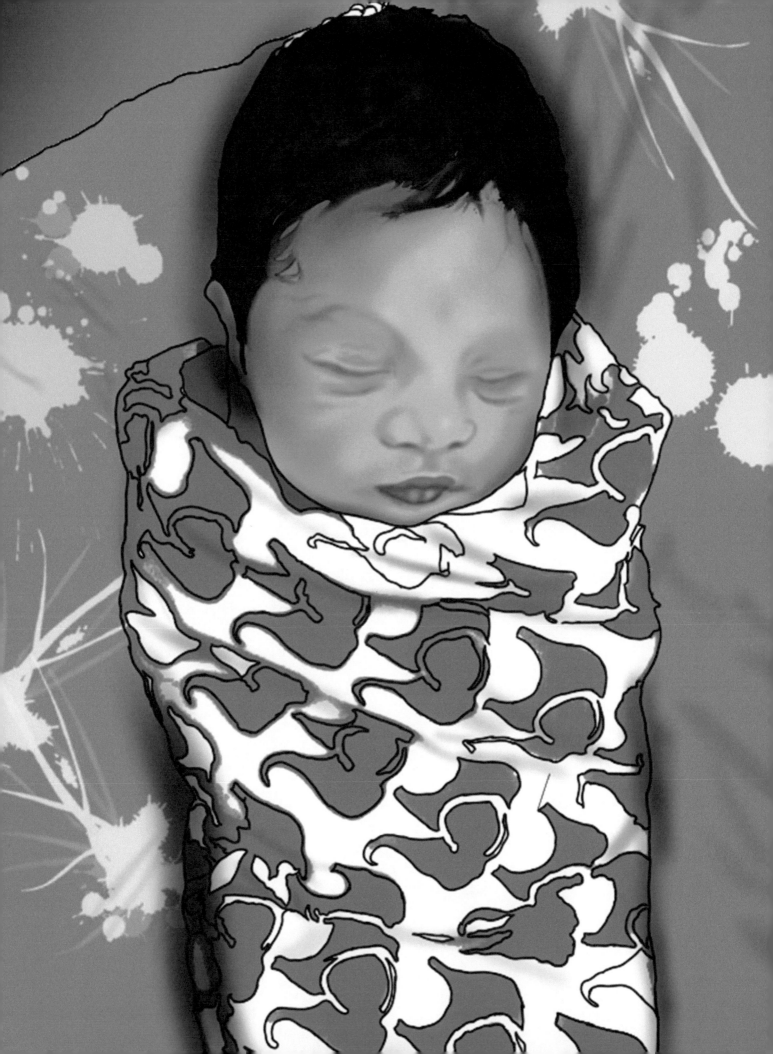

So far in my 365 days of life, I have been on an airplane four times. It's kind of weird sitting down looking at everyone on the plane. For example: some people are sleeping, some are eating, and others won't let me sleep because they keep on talking. When the plane takes off and goes high in the sky, my ears feel kind of weird so dad gives me a pacifier to suck on. He always says, "This will help your ears from ticking."

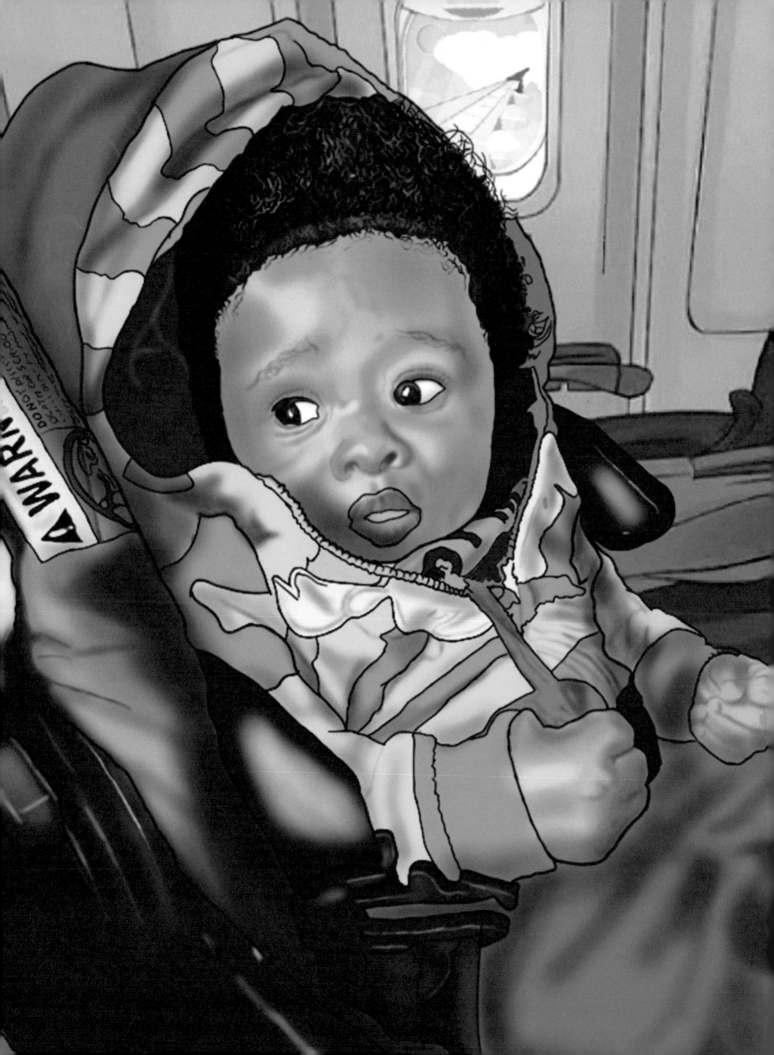

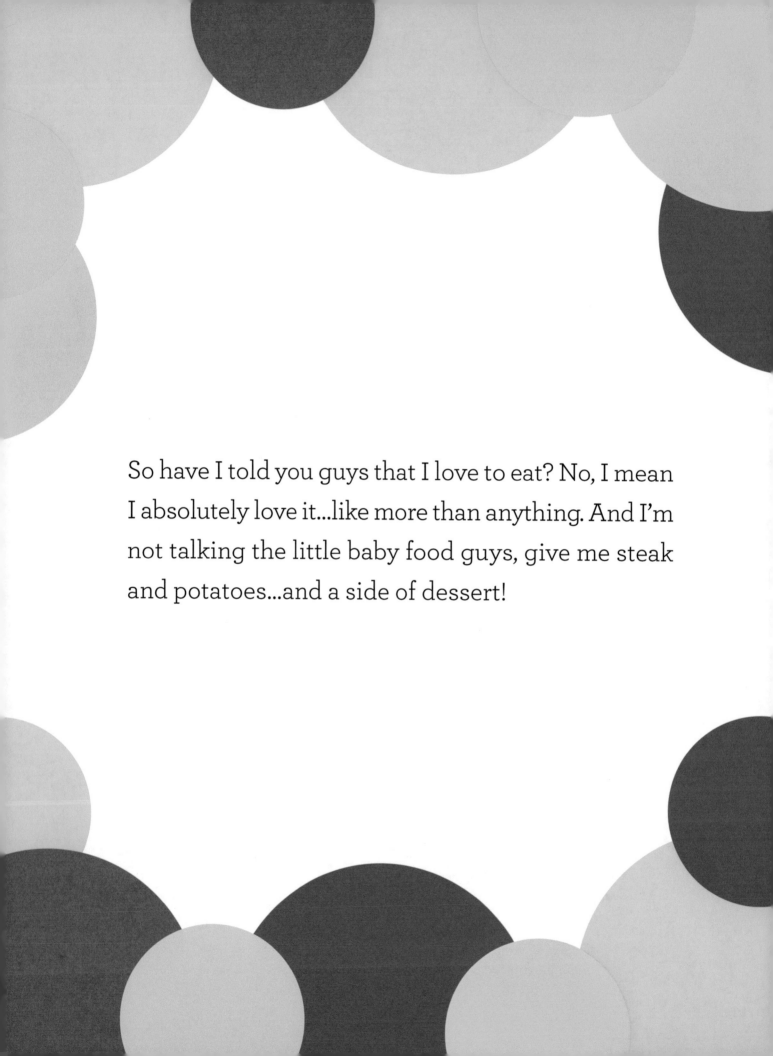

So have I told you guys that I love to eat? No, I mean I absolutely love it...like more than anything. And I'm not talking the little baby food guys, give me steak and potatoes...and a side of dessert!

I'm not much of a crawler; I kind of hate it to be honest. Every time mom puts me on my tummy to crawl, I feel like I'm going to topple over. I like to think of myself as a scooter, that's my preference. I have places to go, and I need to get there fast so put me on my butt and watch me go! Yeah people laugh and think it's kind of cute, but frankly I see nothing funny because I need to get where I'm going fast.

One day I woke up and was told that we were moving, I wasn't really sure what that meant at that time. Mom said we need more room for all my toys, and dad said we needed less space and he placed me in a box. He thought it was very funny, mom and dad laughed forever it seemed. I frankly didn't see the humor in this situation. I looked up at them with my big brown eyes with this look on my face. You'll get use to my look because apparently I do this 90% of the day mom says. She calls me, 'the kid with no expression,' whatever that means.

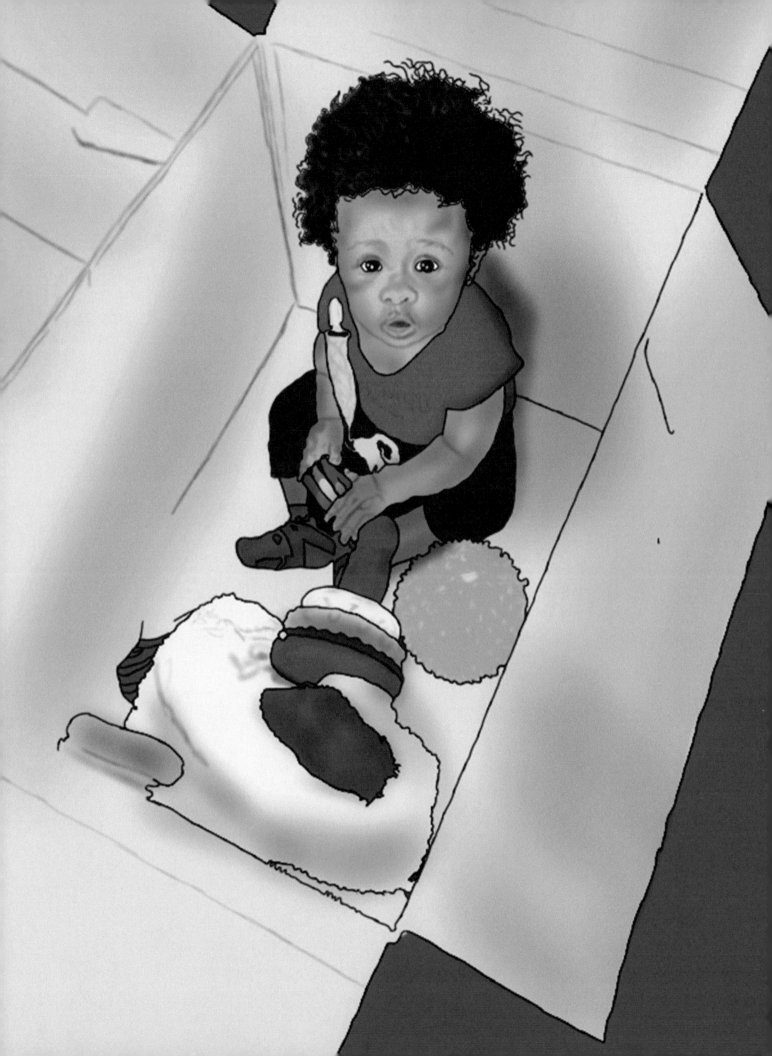

One of the worst things I've ever experienced so far in my first year of life was growing teeth! Did you know that you can actually grow teeth in your mouth? I could barely eat, which made me cry. I could barely sleep, which made me cry. And I was extremely cranky, sorry mom & dad. Thankfully dad gave me a cold toy that I enjoyed chewing on, that was very soothing to my gums.

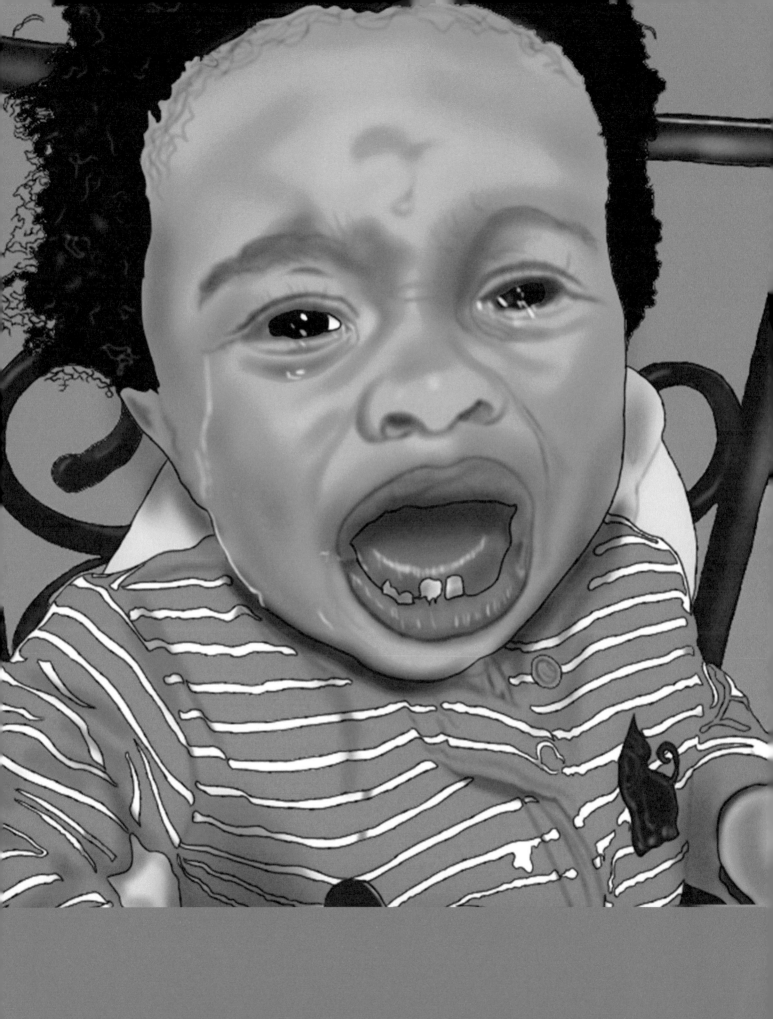

Every so often mom and I go shopping. Shopping is amazing, let mom tell it. We go to the grocery store, where she buys food. We go to clothing stores, where she buys more clothes for the whole family. The only thing I don't like about shopping is we have to drive in the car to get to the store. That is the worst part ever, I hate driving in the car! It's so boring to look at the back seat and watch myself in the mirror. But when mom gives me a bottle, that seems to help.

At first I hated taking baths, hated getting undressed, hated getting my diaper changed...I just hated being completely naked! And when the water touches my skin...I just scream! The older I've become, the more I've come to realize that taking baths really is not so bad. Mom is very gentle when she washes my hair. In fact, it's pretty comforting because she explains everything to me as she is doing it. And now since I'm a big boy, I get to play with toys in the bathtub. Dad sometimes adds little basketball toys to the water, that makes taking baths fun!

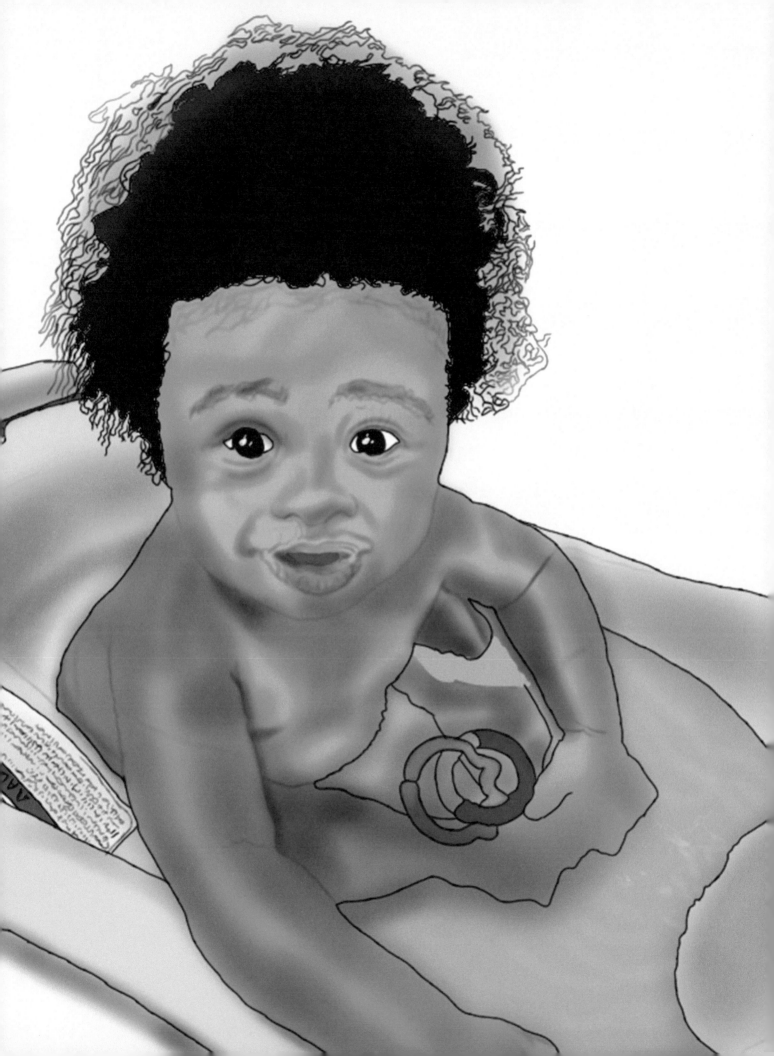

Well guys, that's me in a nutshell. ...Bryson Gregory Melvin. I experienced so much this year. I heard mom and dad say that the fun part is coming next... walking! I use my walker a lot for now, but as I share my next adventure with you...let's see if I can walk without the walker. Until next time my friends, "mom, I think it's time for a snack!"

About the Author

Kendra Carter is originally from Muskegon, Michigan and moved to Las Vegas, Nevada over 6 year ago. A few years back, she was diagnosed with depression slightly before she became pregnant with Bryson. After giving birth to Bryson, she realized he was quite unique. Through everyday experiences with Bryson, she realized life was too precious to sit around and be depressed. She thanks Bryson daily for saving her life and would like to share with the world "Bryson's Big Adventure" one book at a time.

Printed in the United States
By Bookmasters